OUR CHANGING PLANET

Ocean Pollution

Lucy Bashford

Explore other books at:
WWW.ENGAGEBOOKS.COM

VANCOUVER, B.C.

e WWW.ENGAGEBOOKS.COM

Ocean Pollution - Our Changing Planet: *Level 3*
Bashford, Lucy 1958 –
Text © 2023 Engage Books
Design © 2023 Engage Books

Edited by: A.R. Roumanis, Ashley Lee,
Melody Sun & Sarah Harvey
Design by: Mandy Christiansen

Text set in Montserrat Regular.
Chapter headings set in Animated Gothic Light.

FIRST EDITION / FIRST PRINTING

LIBRARY AND ARCHIVES CANADA CATALOGUING IN PUBLICATION

Title: Ocean pollution / Lucy Bashford.
Names: Bashford, Lucy, author.
Description: Series statement: Our changing planet

Identifiers: Canadiana (print) 20230447813 | Canadiana (ebook) 20230447821
ISBN 978-1-77476-994-2 (hardcover)
ISBN 978-1-77476-995-9 (softcover)
ISBN 978-1-77476-996-6 (epub)
ISBN 978-1-77476-997-3 (pdf)
ISBN 978-1-77878-125-4 (audio)

Subjects:
LCSH: Marine pollution—Juvenile literature. |
LCSH: Marine pollution—Prevention—Juvenile literature. |
LCSH: Nature—Effect of human beings on—Juvenile literature.

Classification: LCC GC1090 .B37 2023 | DDC J577.7/27—DC23

This project has been made possible in part
by the Government of Canada.

Canada

Contents

What Is Ocean Pollution?

Pollution is anything that makes Earth unhealthy. Ocean pollution is made up of trash, chemicals, and noise. Most ocean pollution is created by humans.

About 80 percent of ocean pollution comes from the land. It may be blown into the ocean by the wind or carried there by other water sources. The rest of it comes from human activities on the ocean. Old fishing nets are often left behind.

A Closer Look

Some pollution stays near the surface of the ocean. It can collect in large groups called garbage patches. There are five large garbage patches around the world.

There is about thirty times more pollution on the ocean floor than there is on the surface. Scientists have even found garbage in the Mariana Trench. This is the deepest part of the ocean.

Scientists think there are about 5.25 trillion pieces of garbage in the ocean.

What Are Dead Zones?

Dead zones are areas of water where there is little or no oxygen. Plants and animals need oxygen to live. They cannot live in dead zones.

A study done in 2008 found more than 400 dead zones all over the world.

Dead zones are caused by **nutrient pollution**. This pollution can cause a plant called algae to grow and block sunlight from getting to other plants. This causes other plants to die. As they die, the oxygen in the water is used up.

If dead zones are cleaned up, they can support sea life again.

Causes of Ocean Pollution 1

A lot of ocean pollution comes from runoff. Runoff is when rainwater or melting snow picks up **pollutants** from the land and carries them to bodies of water. Common runoff pollutants are oil, gas, animal poop, and chemicals used in farming.

KEY WORD

Pollutants: things that pollute something.

Noise pollution created by humans can make it hard for sea life to live. They depend on sound to find food and other animals. Noise from boats can cause sea life to become sick or stop making babies.

Noise can travel long distances underwater.

Causes of Ocean Pollution 2

Plastic is one of the biggest ocean pollutants. Most plastic pollution comes from single-use plastics. These are things like sandwich bags that are only used once before being thrown away.

By 2050, plastic waste could outweigh all the fish in the oceans.

Plastic does not **decompose** like an apple or banana peel does. It only breaks into tiny pieces called microplastics. Microplastics are less than 0.2 inches (5 millimeters) wide. This means almost all the plastic that has ever been made is still around.

KEY WORD

Decompose: when dead things become a soil-like substance that gives vitamins and minerals to the earth.

Effects on the Planet

Coral reefs are **ecosystems** where lots of sea life live. They need clean, clear water to stay healthy. Pollution is making oceans unclean and causing coral reefs to die. This means sea life can no longer live there.

KEY WORD

Ecosystems: communities of living and nonliving things that work together to stay healthy.

Sea life often gets caught in pieces of garbage. Animals can hurt themselves while trying to get out. They may not be able to get out at all. Some sea life will also try to eat garbage. This can make them sick or kill them.

Old fishing nets are one of the main types of garbage sea life gets caught in.

Effects on Humans

Some sea life can **absorb** chemicals into their bodies. They also eat a lot of microplastics. When people eat seafood, they sometimes eat these chemicals and microplastics as well.

KEY WORD

Absorb: take in or soak up like a sponge.

Lots of ocean pollution ends up on beaches. People do not want to visit dirty beaches. This means businesses near beaches lose customers.

Ocean Pollution Around the World 1

One of the largest oil spills ever happened in 1979. The ships *Atlantic Empress* and *Aegean Caption* hit each other during a storm. About 90 million gallons (340 million liters) of oil were spilled. This is enough to fill more than 136 Olympic-sized swimming pools.

In 2021, a ship called *X-Press Pearl* caught on fire near Sri Lanka. It was carrying dangerous chemicals and containers of tiny plastic pebbles. These chemicals and plastic pebbles all ended up in the ocean.

Ocean Pollution Around the World 2

The Great Pacific Garbage Patch is the largest garbage patch in the world. It is almost three times bigger than France. It can be found between the American states Hawaii and California.

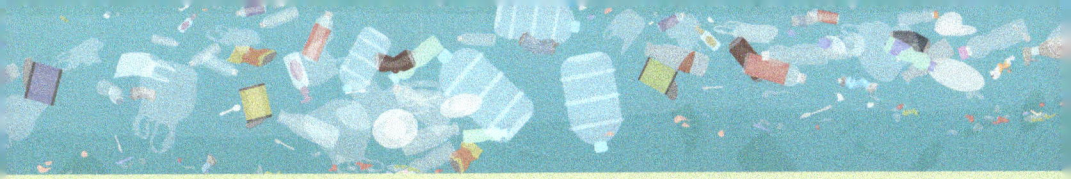

The largest dead zone in the world is in the Arabian Sea. It is bigger than Scotland. It grows as the ocean gets warmer.

Ocean Pollution Solutions 1

Many countries are no longer using some single-use plastics. This means less plastic is being made. It also means less plastic will end up in oceans.

Only about nine percent of plastic is being recycled worldwide.

Some countries have bottle deposit systems. People pay a little bit more when buying drinks. If they take the drink bottles to a recycling center, they get that money back. This helps keep these containers out of oceans.

Norway was one of the first countries to start a bottle deposit system.

Ocean Pollution Solutions 2

Many communities are working together to keep oceans clean. They organize beach cleanups. This keeps the oceans healthy and makes others want to visit their towns.

Scientists are asking shipping companies to find different **routes** that do not cross areas with lots of sea life. They are also asking them to slow their ships down when they do cross over areas with lots of sea life. Ships make less noise when they are moving slower.

25

The Helpers

The Marine Conservation Institute is working to create Marine Protected Areas. These are areas of the ocean that are protected by governments so sea life can stay healthy. Little to no human activity is allowed in these places.

A group called Matter of Trust helps clean up oil spills on **coasts** by making mats out of hair. The hair soaks up the oil so it can be collected safely. They use hair from humans and animals.

KEY WORD

Coasts: areas where the land meets the ocean.

How Can You Help?

If you live near the ocean, help clean up the beaches in your area. Ask your friends to join you. You will have more fun working together.

Try to use less single-use plastics. Find reusable options instead. Use containers instead of sandwich bags. Carry a **reusable** straw with you instead of using a plastic one.

KEY WORD

Reusable: able to be used over and over again.

Quiz

Test your knowledge of ocean pollution by answering the following questions. The questions are based on what you have read in this book. The answers are listed on the bottom of the next page.

1

What is ocean pollution made up of?

2

How many large garbage patches are there around the world?

3

What are dead zones?

4

What are some common runoff pollutants?

5

What is one of the biggest ocean pollutants?

6

In 2021, which ship caught on fire near Sri Lanka?

Explore Other Level 3 Readers.

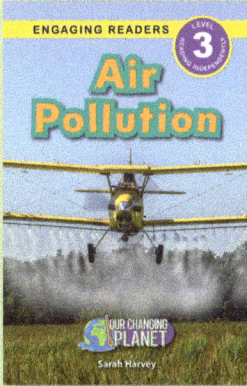

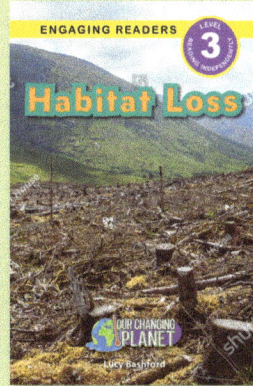

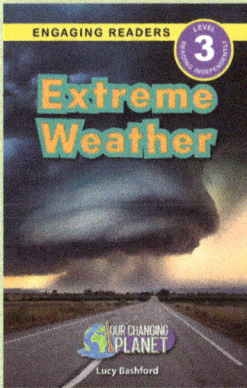

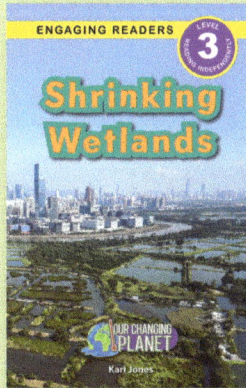

Visit www.engagebooks.com/readers

Answers:
1. Trash, chemicals, and noise 2. Five 3. Areas of water where there is little or no oxygen 4. Oil, gas, animal poop, and chemicals used in farming 5. Plastic 6. A ship called *X-Press Pearl*

www.ingramcontent.com/pod-product-compliance
Lightning Source LLC
Chambersburg PA
CBHW051238020426
42331CB00016B/3438